# Table of Contents

## What are Axolotls?

Axolotls are amphibians that belong to the Caudata family, including salamanders and newts. There are around 8,000 species of amphibians in total, most of which are found in tropical climates. Amphibians have porous skins, and the majority of them have a larval stage, known as a tadpole, which develops from eggs placed in water.

The Axolotl is a salamander species with a particularly distinct genetic composition. It's a paedomorphic salamander that looks like a tiger salamander. They keep most of their larval traits throughout adulthood due to an uncommon condition known as 'neoteny,' thus they exhibit all the characteristics of a tadpole – from feathery gills to a long, quill-like dorsal fin – even when completely developed.

Axolotls, sometimes mistaken for fish, are the only amphibians that spend their whole lives in water. Because of their appearance and preferred environment, axolotls are also known as Mexican walking fish.

The Aztecs discovered a gigantic salamander dwelling in the lake around the island where they established their city, Tenochtitlán when they arrived in the Valley of Mexico in the 13th century. After Xolotl, their deity of fire and lightning, they named the salamander "axolotl." To avoid being sacrificed, Xolotl was claimed to have turned into a salamander, among other forms. He was apprehended and killed in the end.

Axolotls, for example, were routinely killed for food by the Aztecs and are still consumed in Mexico today. They've also become one of the most popular pets globally, owing to their little maintenance and personality. Scientists are interested in organisms because of their exceptional regenerating ability. On the other hand, the salamanders have nearly vanished in their original habitat.

Axolotls should not be confused with the larval stage of the closely related tiger salamander species (A. tigrinum), which are found over most North America and can turn paedomorphic occasionally. They should also not be confused with mudpuppies (Necturus spp.), aquatic salamanders from a separate family that are not closely related to axolotls but look similar.

The Axolotl lived in various lakes across Mexico Valley, but many of its habitats have since dried up and become polluted. Lake Xochimilco and its wetlands are presently the only places where axolotls may be found. Human development, wastewater dumping, habitat loss, and climate change are the leading drivers of Amphibian decline.

Axolotls (Ambystoma mexicanum) belong to the Ambystomatidae family, which has just one extant genus. The Ambystoma genus, sometimes known as mole salamanders, has more than 30 species of salamander. Axolotls may reach a length of 9 inches (20 centimeters) on average, although some have reached more than 12 inches (30 centimeters). Salamanders in captivity live for 5 to 6 years; however, some have survived up to 17 years.
At the age of 18–27 months, a sexually mature adult axolotl can grow to be between 15 and 45 cm (6–18 in) long, with a size of around 23 cm (9 in) being the most frequent and more significant than 30 cm (12 in) being unusual. External gills and a caudal fin that extends from behind the head to the vent distinguish axolotls from salamander larvae. When salamanders reach adulthood, they usually lose their external gills, while the Axolotl retains them. This is due to axolotls' neoteny evolution, which has resulted in their being far more aquatic than other salamander species.

Their eyes are lidless, and their skulls are large. Their limbs are undeveloped, and their digits are lengthy and slender. Males are distinguished by their inflated cloacae coated with papillae, while females are distinguished by their broader bodies, which are filled with eggs. External gill stalks (rami) protrude from behind their heads and are utilized to transport oxygenated water. The external gill rami are laced with filaments (fimbriae). Four-gill slits lined with gill rakers prevent food from entering under the external gills while allowing particles to filter through.

# Why axolotls make great pets

### 1. Axolotls are adorable.
Axolotls are popular pets because of their friendly demeanour. When it comes to these adorable salamanders, there are a variety of hues to pick from. You may have an Axolotl that blooms in the colour of your choice. Albino ones are also famous because of their distinctive red and white colour scheme. It usually is more expensive to purchase a non-albino one. The mottled brown, the melanoid, the golden, and the leucistic, white with red gills and black eyes are also popular variants.
Take a look at GFP Axolotls if you're searching for something unique. They shine under black light, thanks to their altered DNA.

### 2. You don't require a large tank.
A single Axolotl will be more than comfortable in a broad, 20-gallon tank. Because these salamanders live on the ground, it must be enormous. They aren't interested in the tank's upper layers. It is enough for them to spend their time walking on the soft sandy substrate. If you want to keep two Axolotls, you'll need a tank that holds 40 gallons. For one salamander, many owners recommend a 10-gallon tank. However, if you truly want your pet to thrive, you should increase the size by two.
A larger tank also means you won't have to replace the water as regularly.

### 3. There's No Need for a Heater
Axolotls must be kept in a home aquarium with chilly water. The ideal temperature for them is between 61 and 70 degrees Fahrenheit. In light of this, you may need to purchase a cooler if the water in your aquarium is not cold enough. If you don't want to buy one and your home doesn't have chilly places, we recommend keeping your Axolotl in the basement.

## 4. Axolotls are easy to care for.

The Axolotl is the sort of creature who will consume whatever appetising he can get his hands on. It doesn't have to be edible, which is why you shouldn't use a coarse-grained substrate. It would help if you fed them meat-based meals since they are carnivores. Protein is required for them to flourish. Carnivore-specific sinking pellets are ideal for them. Shrimp, bloodworms, and earthworms are also excellent protein sources for them. Pellets mainly designed for Axolotls are also available at most pet stores.

You may feed it with your hand since even if it bites you, it will feel like sandpaper on your skin and will not inflict any damage.

## 5. Axolotls are a peaceful species.

Even though Axolotls are predators, they may appear violent only while attempting to catch their prey. However, they do so out of need, and they are generally relatively calm (especially when domesticated). When they're doing their thing, they usually wander about the aquarium's bottom, investigating. They are calm and peaceful creatures.

If you keep two of them in the same tank, there will be little to no territorial problems. Assuming, of course, that you have purchased a sufficiently sizeable fish tank.

These are just some of the reasons why you should get an Axolotl for your home aquarium. After all, who wouldn't want a pet that is both distinctive and easy to care for? You'll be happy to show off this pet to your friends, whose unique characteristics will enthral.

It's simple to feed them, set up a tank for them, and even breed them. If you want to breed them, you may pick from various hues. Even though Axolotls are generally solitary creatures, you may maintain two of them in one tank or numerous of them in different tanks. When it comes to safety, they are entirely non-poisonous.

# Where do Axolotls live?

Wild axolotls can only be found in the marshy remnants of Lake Xochimilco and the canals that lead to it on Mexico City's southern outskirts. Lake Chalco, another of Mexico City's five "big lakes" where the ancient Aztecs dwelt, once had axolotls as well. According to NBC News, except for Xochimilco, all of those lakes were drained by the 1970s to minimize floods and allow for urban growth.

The carnivorous diet of axolotls has historically placed them at the top of the food chain. Mollusks, fish, and arthropods such as insects and spiders are among the prey they scavenge. Even worse, they consume each other. According to a JSTOR Daily article, the United Nations Food and Agricultural Organization introduced tilapia and carp fish to the salamander's habitat in the 1970s and 1980s to supply residents with more protein. Those fish consume juvenile axolotls and pose a severe threat to salamanders.
Like all other Ambystoma species in Mexico, Axolotls are members of the tiger salamander, or Ambystoma tigrinum, species complex. Like other neotenic species, they live in a high-altitude body of water surrounded by a dangerous terrestrial environment. These circumstances are considered to encourage neoteny. However, in the Axolotl's environment, a terrestrial population of Mexican tiger salamanders lives and breeds.

Due to development in Mexico City and the resulting water pollution, and the introduction of exotic species such as tilapia and perch, wild axolotls were on the verge of extinction by 2020. The International Union for Conservation of Nature and Natural Resources (IUCN) has listed them as critically endangered in the wild, with a declining population of around 50 to 1000 adult individuals. They are listed under Appendix II of the Convention on International Trade in Endangered Species (CITES). Axolotls are frequently utilized in the scientific study because of their capacity to regrow limbs, gills, and sections of their eyes and brains.

# What are the different types of axolotls?

According to estimates, there are currently around 20 distinct varieties of Axolotl hues maintained as pets. Axolotls are undoubtedly one of the prettiest pets you can have. Axolotls may be a strong candidate for the cutest exotic pet ever because of their adorable appearance and creative gills.

In recent years, these little aquatic frogs have become more popular among pet owners worldwide. The species has gotten even more attention because Yolanda Buenaventura was introduced in the famous sitcom Bo Jack Horseman.

The most compelling cause for such interest, though, would be the mind-boggling colour changes, which we will cover in-depth today. Many various colour variants have been developed due to breeding, some of which are rarer and more                                            valuable.

Axolotls receive their colour from two different genes, one from each parent. Each gene is divided into three portions, one for each of the three types of chromatophores (see table above). Alleles are the names for these parts. The number of each chromatophore type generated in the axolotl's epidermis is affected by the combination of alleles, which increases or decreases the colour. An albino person's alleles, for example, code for meagre quantities of melanophores in the skin. Melanophores typically generate a blackish-brown skin tone; however, they are a noticeable white in this person.

The black axolotl is another example. Alleles in melanoid axolotls create more melanophores, resulting in a black species. Some colour patterns can only be seen if an axolotl receives two alleles from both parents.

Axolotls that have one albino allele and one normal allele are not albino. To display albino colour requires two copies of the albino gene. This can make breeding for particular hues more difficult than breeding for others, and it can also affect how rare certain morphs are. Many morphs start with a colour allele mutation, resulting in a unique colour or pattern. This may also happen in snakes, with the Ball Python Morphs being an excellent example. It takes a lot of effort and careful breeding to create a colour morph from a single mutant individual. As the keeping and breeding of this pet become more popular, new forms are continuously being found.

The most popular types are –

## Leucistic

Axolotls with sparkling gold specks, red or pink gills, and dark brown or black eyes are leucistic. They are pretty scarce in the wild because of their vulnerability to predators, yet they are one of the most frequent and attractive variants in captivity. This species resembles albino axolotls in appearance. However, albino axolotls have red eyes.

Leucism is caused by a mutation that causes the skin to generate fewer melanocytes. Axolotls with this mutation do not exhibit the same patterns as the wild-type morph because melanocytes create melanin, a dark pigment.

## Golden Albino

Golden albinos come in various colours, ranging from virtually pure white to peach, yellow, and orange-gold. Their bodies are speckled with shiny dots, and their eyes are white, yellow, or pink. They also have lighter yellow gills that are peachy in colour.

They are indistinguishable from white albinos as youngsters, and they share their sensitivity to bright lights. Only when they grow older do they develop their lovely golden tint. The golden albino variant, like the majority of the light-coloured axolotls on this list, lacks melanophores. This morph is distinct because it contains xanthophores, giving it a golden-yellow hue. Individuals with many iridophores may appear to be coated in gold leaf.

## Wild type

Axolotls in the wild have a dark greyish green colour with black and olive mottling. They also have a light belly and gold speckles from the iridophores. They're the same hues and patterns as wild-caught species. This is the most common and oldest colour in the pet industry.
In 1863, the first wild type species of axolotls were brought to Europe. Depending on the individual, wild axolotls can be virtually black, grey, or a light yellow-green colour. Purple gill filaments and black eyes with golden irises distinguish this variant because their tint may mix with the muddy lakebeds around Mexico City.

## Piebald

Piebalds have dark green, grey, or black symmetrical patches on their face and back, red gills, black eyes, and dark green, grey, or black gills. These patterns can sometimes extend to their sides and legs, although uncommon. This pattern is mainly restricted to the upper portion of the body.

The piebald gene is heritable but highly uncommon, with most breeders based in New Zealand. As the axolotl grows older, this pattern darkens, resulting in a black and white salamander.

This species is a leucistic morph with melanophores concentrated on their heads and backs. The migration of particular cells termed neural crest cells during early development in the egg causes this.

## Mosaic

Mosaic axolotls have black, white, and golden specks on their bodies. They may also have red and purple striped gills and colourful eyes. The majority of mosaics are a mix of melanistic and albino parents.
They're made up of two eggs that have merged into one. Rather than being divided in half, each cell shows colours from both parents at random. This produces a stunning, one-of-a-kind axolotl hue.

Mosaics cannot be bred. They are uncommon and rarely sold, yet they may become accessible on rare occasions.

## Copper

Axolotls with copper-coloured freckles and grey irises have a light grey body. Their gills are greyish-red, and their belly is lighter. Copper axolotls come in various colours, from caramel to nearly pink. This morph is popular in locations where they are sold due to their charming, speckled faces and sandy colouring. Copper axolotls were initially bred in the United States and Australia. Other countries have a more challenging time finding them.
The copper morph is a kind of albinism that is less severe. They have lower melanin and pteridines, although they are not devoid of these pigments. Coppers may be crossed with other morphs to produce unique variations in melanoid copper and axanthic copper.

## Lavender

The lavender axolotl has a faint, silvery purple tint with greyish-red gills and black eyes. Their body is likewise coated with grey patches, thus their Dalmatian name of silver!
Some lavender species mature to a grey or green tint, but most stay purple. Lavender melanoid hybrids, which have a deeper purple hue and no spots, are also produced. This colour combination, however, is relatively uncommon.
Lavender morphs are primarily seen in the United States and have only been produced a few times. Their gentle purple tint and polka-dotted look make them immensely prized despite their scarcity.

## Black Melanoid

This recessive mutation was discovered in a laboratory for the first time in 1961, and it is now rather prevalent. Albinos are the polar opposite of black Melanoids. Melanoid species have fewer iridophores and more melanophores.
They come in various colours, from dark green to entirely black, with dark purple gills. The majority of melanoids also have a grey or purple belly. Some individuals resemble black wild-type axolotls but lack the gleaming golden iris typical in wild axolotls.
Depending on the substrate, black melanoids can vary their colour tones. This colour shift isn't permanent, and your axolotl's colour will fluctuate depending on the substrate. Your axolotl will brighten up using a light substrate like white sand.

## White Albino

White albinos have red gill filaments, pink or white eyes, golden specks on the gill stalks and are entirely white. Young white albinos, especially on their bellies, can be practically transparent. The iridophores on their gills acquire a darker red as they mature, but the rest of their body remains white. There are no xanthophores or melanophores in this species.
Although they have iridophores, these cells are only found in the gills. White albinos resemble leucistic axolotls in appearance, but they lack colour in their eyes. As a result, white albinos are more sensitive to light and have lower vision than other axolotl species.

## Speckled Leucistic

Axolotls with speckled leucistic mutations are one sort of leucistic mutation. They feature dark green, brown, or black speckles on their heads, tails, and backs. Their primary colour is white, much like typical leucistic morphs, and the quantity of speckling isn't as severe as in piebald or mosaic morphs.
This axolotl frequently looks like a leucistic at first and then develops speckling later in life. Their pigment cells develop as they grow, allowing them to modify their hue and freckle pattern.

## Chimera

Because the Chimera is so uncommon, it is debatable whether it should be recognised as a real morph. Chimeras have two morphs on one half of their bodies and one on the other. It is divided into two halves, one on the left and one on the right. Half albino and half wild-type chimaeras have been born thus far. Chimera axolotls are formed when two developing eggs combine to become one. Since the two eggs did not fuse entirely, most do not hatch.
Chimeras cannot be selectively bred since they are a developmental mishap that is not caused by genetics.

## Heavily-Marked Melanoid

The heavily-marked melanoid morph is a distinct variety of the black melanoid.
Normal black melanoids feature black and purplish-grey dots containing light green and yellow patches. This mutation has only been observed a few times, and nothing is known about it. Because it's impossible to anticipate whether two melanoid parents would generate strongly marked offspring, these colour variants are uncommon.

## Green Fluorescent Protein

At first glance, Green Fluorescent Protein axolotls appear to be any other morph. However, when exposed to UV radiation, they turn a dazzling fluorescent green. In average daylight, this feature is undetectable, but in UV light, it is apparent. Those with lighter skin, such as albino or leucistic people, have a more flawless glow.
The green fluorescent protein gene was discovered in jellyfish and intentionally transferred into the axolotl genome. Researchers at the Max Planck Institute generated this morph in 2005 to examine cellular mobility and cancer.

## Firefly

Lloyd Strohl invented the Firefly axolotls as an intentionally manufactured morph. Embryonic graphing was first used to research limb regeneration, and there is some debate regarding whether or not it should be utilised to generate pets.
Because the firefly feature must be developed in a lab, they are scarce. They're dark-coloured wild-type axolotls with albino tails of a green fluorescent protein. Because just a portion of the body glows under a blacklight, they are dubbed "fireflies." Like a firefly, a wild-type with an albino tail will shine bright green on only the tail.

## Enigma

Dark grey with a white belly and toes, pale red gills, and golden eyes, the Enigma morph is mysterious. It's coated with gleaming golden spots that, from some perspectives, resemble green. A breeder in the United States originally discovered this one-of-a-kind axolotl.
It is an axolotl of the wild kind with many iridophores. There is just one enigma at the moment, and little is known about its genetics or heredity.

## How to distinguish between a male and female axolotl?

One of the fascinating aspects of axolotls is that the gender of the axolotl is challenging to determine. Only a few changes exist between male and female axolotls. As a result, you may want to pay special attention to telling them apart based on their gender. While male and female axolotls may appear reasonably identical, particular distinctions can help you tell them apart.

To begin with, their bodily forms are dissimilar. Females have rounder bodies than men because they are expected to carry eggs, and their bodies have evolved to accommodate this reality. On the other hand, Males have a considerably longer and straighter physique, making them appear leaner and more attractive.

The lower down you look at a woman's abdomen, the broader she becomes. They take on a "pear form" as a result of this. A female axolotl produces eggs regularly then reabsorbs them if no male spawns with her. Regardless of the egg cycle stage, her form remains more rounded than the males.

Males also have a longer tail than females, which is reflected in the elongated curve of their bodies and their total length. These are the two most essential differences in determining whether your axolotl is male or female.

You may also tell the difference between male and female axolotls by glancing at their cloaca (vent). The most significant difference is that males have a significantly more clear vent, which stands out more because it is swollen. Females have only a slight hump in this location if they have any alteration in their bodies at all.

On the other hand, females may experience something known as a "poop bump," which causes it to become more significant than usual. Instead of bulging out to the sides, the faeces bump causes the region to sink in a sharp "V" or softer "U" shape. If you compare it to the male's cloaca, you can tell the difference.

After the axolotl has gone to the toilet, the region returns to average and flat, indicating a poop bump. Male axolotls develop a bulge behind their rear legs and reach sexual maturity. The amount of this protrusion varies from axolotl to axolotl, but it is always noticeable. Males vary in their "obviousness." Some are more "obvious" than others. The bulge often gets considerably more pronounced and flushed during the breeding season.

## What Are the Uncommon and Rare Axolotl Morphs?

Due to its rarity, GFP Axolotls are a popular favorite among Axolotl owners. This morph is rare, yet it's simple to come by because GFP Axolotls are popular to breed. Any Axolotl that has been genetically edited to carry the Green Fluorescent Protein Gene is known as a GFP Axolotl. Due to this protein synthesis, GFP Axolotls can glow green under UV light. GFP resembles a secondary morph.

There is no such thing as a GFP Axolotl. One of the other morphs has to be the Axolotl. You can have a GFP Leucistic Axolotl, for example. The GFP gene may be passed down through the generations, and lighter-colored Axolotls containing the gene shine brighter.

Due to the red hue in their eyes, Copper Morphs are often mistaken for Albino Axolotls. They usually are light brown and have dark brown markings. This morph is typically more challenging to locate than the others.

Chimera Axolotls are Axolotls that result from the fusion of two eggs. This can result in an Axolotl with one morph on one half of its body and another on the other. There is a divide in the colours. Because one side of a chimaera Axolotl might develop faster than the other, it is exceedingly improbable to survive. It isn't easy to purposefully breed this morph.

Mosaic Morphs are pretty similar to chimaera Axolotls in that they are a blend of two morphs, but they aren't precisely divided in half. Most mosaics are sterile because they are made up of two cells that arise throughout development. It's also not possible to purposefully breed the morph.

Piebald Morphs are leucistics with darker pigmentation on the sides of their bodies and the tops of their heads. Compared to typical Axolotls with spots, their spots are darker and fuller. This morph color can be passed down over the generations.

The Lavender Morph is another option. This morph can be challenging to come by. Axolotls with a purple hue and black markings are known as lavender morphs.

Only one breeder can acquire Firefly Morphs, who can use the breed for research and then sell them. Using embryonic graphing, Lloyd Stroh II constructed this unique morph. Regular breeding will not produce the morph. Axolotls with a light tail have a dark tail, whereas those with a dark tail have a light tail.

# What to know before buying them?

The axolotl, a sort of aquatic salamander, is undoubtedly a one-of-a-kind pet. They do not undergo a metamorphosis from larval to adult form when their respiration shifts from gills to lungs, as do most salamanders. Instead, they spend their whole lives in the water. As a result, you do not handle them, but they may be rather interesting to observe. They are generally easy to care for and resilient, making them a good choice for first-time pet owners. Furthermore, their nutritional requirements are simple.

Things to know before buying them –

1. Make Sure Axolotls Are Legal to Own Where You Live Axolotls aren't allowed to be kept as pets in every country or state in the United States. So, if you want such a pet, make sure it's legal where you live first. Axolotls are illegal in California, New Jersey, Virginia, and Maine as of the writing of this book. However, because these laws are prone to change, you should always double-check to see which exotic pets are acceptable in your country/state.
The fact that axolotls are an endangered species is one of the main reasons they are forbidden to import in many countries. That's why we always advocate buying an axolotl as a pet from a breeder rather than a wild-caught axolotl — you don't want to contribute to the species' demise. As a result, states and nations owning axolotls are lawful, but importing them from another state or country is prohibited. Axolotls make excellent pets since they are so well-behaved.

Axolotls are excellent pets, not just because of their appearance but also their disposition. These aquatic reptiles are mild-mannered and quiet, and they like swimming, hiding and playing about their tank's plants and decorations, as well as peering through the glass at you while you're viewing them.

On the other hand, Axolotls aren't precisely friendly, which may be both a benefit and a drawback depending on your preferences. In their tanks, axolotls don't mind being alone. They prefer it. They don't mind if you break the glass or cause a commotion around it, but they don't like being handled.

This final point is critical given that axolotls are incredibly gentle creatures. Because axolotls are so delicate, most of their skeletal system is formed of cartilage rather than bone. Handling axolotls is, therefore, typically unwise and should be avoided. It's recommended to use a fine mesh net to relocate your axolotl from or into its tank. This will make the transition seamless, simple, and safe - as long as the mesh is fine enough that the axolotl's limbs do not become entangled in it.

2. Axolotls have amazing regenerative capabilities

When assaulted, several reptiles and lizards are reported to remove their tails and grow a new one afterwards. Axolotls can accomplish all of this and more! Other limbs and even bodily components can regenerate in these cute Mexican salamanders, such as the heart and eye tissue!

Of course, this doesn't imply you should annoy them excessively or put them in circumstances where they can suffer limb harm. The ability to regenerate a tail or a foot does not imply good health. Another reason to avoid housing your axolotl or another pet is that you should only gather two axolotls together if you're very positive they'll get along.

3. Get the right axolotl from the right breeder

Axolotls are pretty easy to obtain from fellow breeders and online. It is recommended to opt for a captive-bred axolotl over a wild-caught one in any case. Axolotls are already endangered in their natural habitat; therefore, obtaining wild-caught specimens will only hasten their extinction.

Furthermore, captive-bred axolotls make superior pets like other reptiles and exotic pets. They are more habituated to life in an aquarium, are used to artificial lighting, and are unconcerned about being surrounded by people.

Furthermore, if the axolotl is a captive-bred pet, a breeder should be able to provide you with essential health information on the axolotl and its parents. This is quite useful if you want a healthy pet even though axolotls generally don't have too many health issues – more on that below.

4. A good aquarium is the first thing you'll need to get for your future axolotl

You should get the tank and set it up before you get your pet or even before ordering it to be delivered. Axolotls have some exact environmental requirements, despite how easy they are to care for. This implies that everything has to be in place before your axolotl comes into your house.

So, what size tank should the axolotl have?

A 10-gallon tank is a bare minimum for a single axolotl. However, if you want your pet to be happy and comfortable, we recommend something more significant. A minimum of 20 litres is suggested, mainly because axolotls deposit their faeces in the water they swim in. An adult axolotl may reach 12 inches (30 cm) and weigh up to 10 ounces (300 grams).

As a result, the more extensive the tank, the cleaner the water will be between repairs. And, if you plan on caring for more than one axolotl, you'll need a larger tank. We recommend a minimum of 30-40 litres for two axolotls.

The tank itself may be any standard glass tank - as long as the glass is robust enough to withstand the weight of the water within, you should be OK. As with other aquarium creatures, you'll want to install a sound filtration system in the tank.

Indeed, you should ensure that the filtration system is as effective as possible, as axolotls create more waste than fish, necessitating more excellent filtering and more regular filter changes. However, make sure the filter isn't too powerful because strong water currents might stress your axolotl.

The aquarium's contents may be filled with water because axolotls are purely aquatic and never need to leave the water. However, because axolotls do occasionally try to escape the water, a mesh should be firmly installed over the tank to prevent the reptile from leaping out.

Last but not least, the interior of the tank. This may be kept basic and tailored to your preferences. Of course, the tank's bottom shouldn't be all glass, but a layer of regular aquarium sand should suffice. However, some axolotl owners advocate using gravel bigger than the reptile's head to avoid the axolotl unintentionally eating it.

5. Set up the right lighting

The first thing to remember is that axolotls dislike bright lights when it comes to illumination. As a result, the aquarium for your axolotl should be located away from any sources of direct and bright light. This involves keeping the aquarium away from any windows, as well as any very bright lights. This isn't to say that the room should be gloomy all of the time; you may certainly switch on the lights in the evening. They should, however, not be excessively bright, and they should not be placed immediately next to or above the axolotl's tank.

6. Keep your axolotl healthy

Axolotls have extraordinary regeneration abilities, but that does not imply they are immune to illness. If you haven't maintained your axolotl's tank clean enough, for example, viral and bacterial illnesses are a common concern.

Another issue to be aware of is ammonia accumulation, which may be harmful. Look for gastrointestinal blockages if your axolotl has eaten the little pebbles or sand at the bottom of the tank. Sluggishness and a lack of appetite are common symptoms.

# Best places to buy them

Axolotls are amphibious organisms that can breathe via their gills and lungs; nevertheless, they cannot survive on land and must be submerged. This is owing to their cartilage-based bodies, which are pliable. This makes them sensitive to objects that create abrasions on the skin, such as crawling on the ground, especially at a young age.
Axolotls have a slime covering their whole body, protecting the outside world. When the axolotl is out of the water, its slime coat dries off, exposing the axolotl's fragile skin to the perils of the world.

Furthermore, an axolotl's skin is light-sensitive, and water serves to diffuse the light that would otherwise strike the axolotl. Overall, the axolotl's native environment in the wild is in the water, so don't separate them from it.

It also implies you shouldn't touch your axolotl since it will cause more damage than good. As a result, treat axolotls as if they were fish. You can't pet it; you can only stare at it. When it comes to the axolotl's habitat, you'll want to pay careful attention to the tank size, the gravel you use in the tank, the filter you acquire for the tank, and the extra shelter you'll need to offer it in the tank.

It is recommended that a first-time customer purchase an Axolotl in person. You may not only see what you're getting in person, but you might also get some great advice.
Because axolotls must be kept at a cold temperature of 16-18° C, few lizard or reptile businesses carry them. If someone asks where to get them, axolotls may only be purchased from axolotl enthusiasts or private aquatic pet breeders. If you're unsure where to get an axolotl, check with your local authorities to see if it's legal to keep one as a pet.

Look for states like Florida that allow axolotls to be cared for. After that, you'll need to seek axolotls for sale. Choose the sort of axolotl you want in Florida.

The second-best location to get axolotl is on the internet. Axolotl may be found at various online retail outlets at reasonable costs. Make sure you choose a reputable website that sells amphibians. Check the website's legitimacy and customer reviews to ensure it is not a fraud. Scammers create online eCommerce businesses for fraudulent purposes, and there are plenty of them on the internet these days. The finest axolotl dealer is one who raises the amphibians. You'll get the most outstanding value if you can discover someone who breeds them from eggs till they mature.

# Behaviour and Socialisation among Axolotls

Axolotls, contrary to common perception, do not gain from socialization. As a result, they thrive in their seclusion. Because of their severe cannibalistic instincts, axolotls should be kept separate until they are at least 5 inches long.

The axolotls usually are grown enough at 5 inches to overcome their cannibalism. If you notice any symptoms of one axolotl injuring another in the cage, separate them as soon as possible. This way, you won't have to worry about one axolotl injuring the other.

Because axolotls have a remarkable ability to regenerate, separating them before any substantial harm is done will likely allow both axolotls to mend and survive the encounter.

The advantage of having two axolotls together is that you can breed them if their genders are opposite.

Other watery species should not be kept in the same tank as the axolotl. Because of the axolotl's fragile skin, any creature that enters the tank and nibbles at the axolotl might do considerable injury.

Let the axolotl alone to avoid this. If necessary, you can drop their food into the tank when hungry, but you should typically leave them alone.

**Tips for axolotl socialization –**

**Tip #1**: By the time they reach a full body size of 3.5 to 4 inches, most axolotls will have grown out of their cannibal phase. Make careful to put axolotls of equal size together. Whether in a cannibal phase or not, if one's head fits inside the others, its food!

**Tip #2**: Pick a period when both axolotls appear comfortable, healthy and stuffed. It's critical to feed them ahead of time properly!

**Tip #3:** A protein-deficient axolotl is more prone to bite tankmates regardless of age or other factors. If your axolotl is a rescue, give them a couple of weeks of good nourishment before introducing them to your other axolotls.

**Tip #4**: Keep an eye on the initial interaction and prepare to separate if necessary. It's OK to invade each other's personal space. It's OK to sniff each other. It's also natural to be a little jittery. Prepare to interfere if you see someone striding towards the other with their nose to the ground since this is a bite waiting to happen. Snapping directly in front of each other's faces is more of a danger, but it's still a warning that the axolotl isn't ready to share its tank with another animal. Separate them and give them another shot in a few weeks.

**Tip #5**: If everything goes smoothly for the first few minutes, keep an eye on the baby throughout feeding time during the first few days. That's when violent behaviour frequently emerges. Feed them in different tank regions so that they don't eat each other's food. Food should not be taken from each other since it breeds aggression. It's also not a good idea to snap near each other's limbs, so don't allow the food to go too close to someone's toes. Feed the most food-aggressive axolotls first, then feed the more timid ones away from the hungry ones.

**Tip #6**: If you observe that one axolotl hides a lot, refuses to come out at feeding time, and avoids food, they are either unwell or afraid of a food-aggressive tankmate. Separate the animals and try again once they appear happy and healthy.

**Tip #7**: Don't be disheartened if a couple doesn't get along immediately away. Remove them from each other and try again in a few weeks. It doesn't imply it won't work out next time just because it didn't work out the first time.

# What should be suitable water temp and ph.?

Axolotls do best in their tanks, and any tank sharing poses a risk. Young axolotls can be housed together if there is enough space, and while adult axolotls are less likely to cannibalism, those of different sizes should not be kept together.
It's critical to get the pH of the water in your axolotl tank to the right level for the health of your amphibian pets. The alkalinity or acidity of your water is measured by its pH. Axolotls can survive in water with a pH of 6.5 to 8.0, although their optimal pH is 7.4–7.6. Ammonia poisoning, which can be lethal to your axolotl, can occur if the pH of the waterfalls beyond the acceptable range.
Chlorine, which may be present in tap water, is toxic to axolotls, so either uses a de-chlorinator or let the water sit for 24 hours before adding it to the tank. A dechlorinator is required if you reside in a region where chloramines are added to the water. Every week, 10-20% of the water should be replaced. However, this might vary based on the tank's filter system.

## Why is pH Important?
The toxicity of ammonia, a potentially lethal toxin, may be affected by the pH level of your water, especially if it reaches high amounts and is left unchecked.
Water with a pH of 7 is regarded as neutral. It's acidic if it's below 7 and essential if it's above 7. Returning to the optimal pH values for axolotls, which are about 7.4–7.6, we may deduce that axolotls enjoy somewhat essential water.
To minimize ammonia toxicity to a minimum, keep the pH of the water in the tank within the optimal range for axolotls. It's also critical to ensure that the pH levels remain constant.

## How to Measure pH?

Regular testing is the only method to maintain the pH level in the aquarium steady. The simplest method to do this is to use aquarium testing kits, which can check for various factors like pH and toxins.

Periodic testing ensures that you can keep a close eye on water parameters and make modifications as needed.

## How to Adjust Water pH?

So, you've been testing your water and noticed that the pH level is getting near to being outside the limit that axolotls can tolerate. When this happens, depending on the result of the testing strip, you can adjust the pH level up or down. pH Up and pH Down are two separate additives that can reduce or raise the pH level, depending on the scenario. However, it's vital to modify the pH gradually and avoid making drastic changes since these can also harm your axolotls. You'll need to make minor adjustments and gradually boost the pH levels to avoid straining your axolotls. Continue adjusting until you obtain the desired result.

# Axolotl Water Temperature Requirements

Another crucial water parameter that aquarists must manage within acceptable limits is water temperature. Because axolotls are sensitive to temperature changes, you must maintain a constant water temperature. Axolotls can endure water temperatures between 59- and 73-degrees Fahrenheit (15 and 23 degrees Celsius). The recommended water temperature ranges from 60 to 64 degrees Fahrenheit (16 and 18 degrees Celsius).
Variations in water temperature and water beyond the allowed range for axolotls can have a variety of negative repercussions, including an increased risk of illnesses like fungal infections, a lack of appetite, decreased movement, and a variety of other factors problems that can lead to death.

## Which is worse for Axolotls – Warm Water or Cold Water?

Axolotls do best in cooler water, but not too cold. Warmer water beyond their tolerable range is very hazardous for them. Warm water can speed up their metabolism, resulting in increased food intake and waste output, raising the ammonia content in the tank. Warm water also has a lower oxygen content. All of these things can cause germs to flourish and fungus to increase, resulting in illnesses and disorders, some of which can be fatal to your axolotl.
You may have observed that axolotls prefer cooler water by looking at their preferred temperature range. Of course, too cold water is unpleasant, but it isn't quite as horrible as water that is too hot.

Cold water causes their metabolism to slow down, resulting in decreased movement and a loss of hunger. While keeping your axolotl in cold water isn't as awful as keeping them in hot water, you should still strive for the optimal range to keep your axolotl healthy.
Cooling down the water for axolotls is a considerably greater issue for most aquarists than making sure it's warm enough.

# How to decorate the tank and make them feel in their own habitat

Setting up an Axolotl tank necessitates meticulous preparation ahead of time. You can ensure that this little salamander remains happy and healthy by providing the proper circumstances. For example, you can't just place an Axolotl in an uncycled tank. It must be cycled, and all preparations must be completed appropriately.

Things to note –

## Substrate for Axolotl

It would help if you used sand substrate in your tank to minimise impaction. Axolotls are bottom dwellers, which means they spend most of their time on the substrate. This is why it's critical to select the appropriate substrate for your pet. Others may advise you to keep your Axolotl in a tank without substrate.

Although this isn't always a terrible alternative, many specialists believe that the lack of footing may cause stress to your pet. If you want a bare-bottom tank, the best option is to lay down some tile or slate. Either of them can help your Axolotl get a better grip. When these salamanders are hungry, they devour anything of that size to avoid abrasive substrate.

## Live Plants

Axolotls have several interesting behaviors, one of which is that they enjoy perching on plants. This is too much for weaker plants to handle. They frequently shatter under their weight, which is why you should opt for more durable ones. A few robust live plants will work well with your Axolotl.

Among them are Java Fern, Eludia, Marimo moss ball, and floating plants such as Amazon Frogbits and Water Lettuce. The issue with Eludia is that it grows pretty quickly, so keep that in mind. All of these plants are attractive, and they'll make your aquarium appear vibrant and alive.
But, more significantly, they will not be uprooted or broken. Considering that Axolotls demand frigid water temperatures, it's astonishing that they may even be found among plants.

## Hides for Axolotls

Instead of rock caves and other natural hiding places, Axolotls prefer porcelain objects. Just make sure there aren't any rough edges on which your pet might be wounded. In a pet store, you may get various beautiful and natural-looking ones.

Axolotl owners commonly purchase cichlid rocks or ceramic pipes. These salamanders must have hiding areas where they may retreat. Otherwise, they may get stressed and intimidated.

## Driftwood

Driftwood is also an excellent option. You may place a number of them in an Axolotl cage, and the little guy will be delighted. The same is true of driftwood with the pottery object we discussed before. You should choose ones with no sharp edges so that your pet does not injure himself. By adding a few pieces of driftwood to your aquarium, you may make it appear even more natural.

It's usually a good idea to double-check a piece because it may have irregular edges that you don't see at first. Mopani and Cholla Wood are the best sorts of driftwood to use. These will look fantastic when paired with plants, as well as on their alone.

## Rocks

In your Axolotl tank, a few larger rocks can be used as décor. Rocks come in such a wide variety of forms and colours that you may customize the aquarium to your preferences.

They must be large enough to avoid being swallowed by your Axolotl, which will result in a bad outcome.

There are always lovely dragon stones or river rocks to choose from when it comes to rocks. It's critical to seek those who don't dissolve any metals in aquarium water. Axolotls, for example, can be poisoned by calcium.

If you're not confident about seeking rocks in the wild, you can always go to the pet store and purchase some ornamental ones.

## Aquarium Decorations

As you might have guessed from the examples above, the goal is to avoid using sharp items. To make it appear distinctive, you can always discover some safe aquarium decorations.

This is where you may let your imagination go wild since the choices for decorating are virtually unlimited. In the end, almost every piece of aquarium décor will serve as a potential hiding spot, which your Axolotl will like.
Even while not every form of decorating suits them, there are still many options. If you enjoy being creative and experimenting with colours, you will be able to create a stunning tank.

## Aquarium Equipment

Aside from aquarium decorations and hideouts, your axolotl tank will require some equipment. The most crucial thing is to have a decent aquarium filter in your axolotl's tank to keep the ammonia and nitrate levels in check.
Because a good filter will dissolve enough oxygen in the water, an air pump is not required for your axolotl tank.
On the other hand, an aquarium chiller may be required to keep the water in your tank cold. Axolotls like colder water, preferring temperatures of 60-64 °C (16-18 °C), thus if the ambient temperature is higher than these, you should chill the water.

## Tank Cleaning

Axolotls are cute, so make them feel at ease when you bring them home. They're simple to care for, and if you keep them in the appropriate climate, you'll be able to enjoy them for up to 15 years. In addition to providing healthy nutrition, they require a healthy environment. If you're raising them in tanks, make sure the tanks are clean since filthy water can lead to bacterial diseases.

How often should your axolotl tank be cleaned? Veterinary advice is usually given within a fortnight, although it might be given more often. If you have more axolotls in your tank, there will be more waste, and you need to change your water more frequently.

In a 10-gallon tank, for example, only maintain two adult axolotls. Remove any uneaten food and feces daily. Axolotl excrement produces ammonia, whereas decomposing food residues include nitrates, which break down into nitrites, toxic to axolotls.

90% of Nitrate, Nitrite, and Ammonia are removed when the water is changed often (at least once a week). As a result, the concentration of these compounds will seldom ever reach dangerous levels.

The above pattern is recommended for small tank water changes, but what if you have significant water tanks?

To help you understand when to change the water, consider these 5 factors:

- The filter strength
- Tank's size
- Feeding
- Age and size of your axolotls
- Number of axolotls

If you have fewer axolotls and keep them in larger tanks, there will be less concentration and ample aeration, and if your filter is in good working order, you may replace the water after one to several months. If you don't replace the water, the pH and KH will drop (making the water more acidic) as the nitrate levels grow, and your axolotls may get Old Tank Syndrome. If this happens, the pets may perish, and if you want to raise them again, you'll need to replace the water.

A water change of roughly 20-25% each week (in combination with water testing) is a good rule of thumb for tank cleaning. Remember to use a water conditioner to eliminate chlorine/chlorinates from the water before using it. They have the potential to disrupt your nitrogen cycle. The water change should help you maintain a healthy nitrate level while also keeping your axolotls happy and healthy.

Never empty and scrub your tank; this will cause the tank to lose its cycle, and you will have to start over. To begin, you'll need to get a decent gravel vacuum to remove the trash properly. This will save you a lot of time and work when cleaning up trash and leftover meals.

If you're using a syphon, the end of the syphon goes into the bucket to capture the water that's being sucked out; if you're using a tap-attached aquarium vacuum, the water flows down the drain. It would help if you started cleaning by getting rid of the trash first. Begin by sucking out all of the pop and other waste in the tank by simply passing the waste product over it and letting it be sucked out. After you've removed all of the waste but haven't removed 25% of the water, leave the syphon in the water until 25% of the water has been removed.

# Diet – what to feed and what not to

There are various types of food for axolotls.

However, because axolotls are carnivores, it is critical to understand that they eat nearly anything they may discover in their environment.

Axolotls eat minute insects, such as worms, fish, larvae, and mollusks, in their native environment.

Nightcrawlers, blackworms, daphnia, raw meat, brine shrimp, and pellets are the finest foods to feed your axolotl in captivity. Reptile live food, which includes a variety of worms, is the greatest nutritional meal you'll ever discover for your exotic pets.

Before we go any further, let's go through the many types of axolotl food:

## Nightcrawlers (Large Earthworms)

Nightcrawlers are without a doubt the most nutritious and everyday axolotl meal available. They are also conveniently available from anywhere. Canadian nightcrawlers, European nightcrawlers, and red wigglers are typical for axolotls. The Canadian and European Nightcrawlers are the most popular in terms of nutritional value. On the other hand, red wiggler worms are more prevalent because they are easier to produce and smaller than other night crawlers.

## Blackworms

For young axolotls, blackworms are an excellent replacement for nightcrawlers. Blackworms, like nightcrawlers, are widely accessible and provide a good source of protein. However, I still do not suggest them because they make a massive mess in your aquarium and necessitate extensive cleaning regularly. The remaining blackworms wreak havoc in the tank, creating a breeding ground for germs in your axolotl aquarium.

## Blood worms

Many axolotl owners choose bloodworms as a food source. Fly larvae or sea worms can be given to them. In whatever shape they take, bloodworms are not as nutritious as other worm species. As a result, I propose regularly giving bloodworms to adult and young axolotls as a reward. Bloodworms can make a lot of trash in your axolotl tank, and if left in water for too long, they might develop fungus. To accommodate this, I recommend keeping bloodworms in a large container. The worms would not spread around the tank and poison the water this way.

## Daphnia

Daphnia is rich in fatty acids, lipids, and other vital vitamins that help your larval or infant axolotls develop well. Although adult axolotls like eating Daphnia, they are unlikely to supply enough nourishment for your axolotls, leaving them hungry and continually seeking more. This leads to more frequent feedings and a poor diet. However, live food, such as Daphnia and worms, might bring illnesses and parasites, which could hurt your axolotl. As a result, I advocate purchasing your pet's food from trusted sources or cultivating it yourself.

## Baby Brine Shrimp

If live daphnia isn't accessible for your newborn axolotl, brine shrimps can be added to the diet. They're a good source of vitamins, lipids, and fatty acids for your axolotl. On the other hand, the young brine shrimp may not always reach your happy little axolotl. I propose using Turkey baster for this, and your axolotls will be fine. Remove any squandered brine shrimps, dead naupilen, or newly developed larvae, which produce a terrible odor and muddy the water. Brine Shrimp may be hatched and raised at home. So, if you'd instead offer them to your Axolotls as a live meal rather than frozen, that's OK too. Brine shrimps, like live daphnia, can carry diseases. As a result, it is essential to get them from reliable retailers or to breed them at home.

# Lifespan and health

In captivity, axolotls typically live for 10-15 years, but they may survive for over 20 years when well cared for. The oldest axolotl is unknown, but their age might surprise them if they become more frequent pets as some salamander species have exceptionally lengthy lifespans. Though the axolotl is a little salamander with a short lifespan, they survive longer than many people think when they acquire them as pets! Their capacity to regenerate bodily parts like limbs and even organs contributes to their resiliency.

Axolotls live in captivity for 10-15 years and 5-10 years in the wild. What factors contribute to such a significant disparity in lifespan?

Predators, sickness, and habitat loss are challenges to these salamanders in their natural environment. Captive life, on the other hand, isn't always easy. Axolotls, like many other exotic pets, are routinely neglected.

## Predators

Axolotls don't have a lot of self-defense abilities. They have no fangs or claws and move slowly. In the wild, this makes them easy prey for predators. Invasive species imported to its natural area have also preyed on axolotls.

## Pollution

The axolotl population has suffered due to its tiny native habitat in the lakes surrounding Mexico City. Due to water contamination, the species was on the verge of extinction in 2010, and it remains vulnerable in the wild today.

# Health Issues

Fluid build-up, tumors, germs, fungus, and parasites are among health concerns for axolotls. Inbreeding is to blame for some of the axolotl's health issues. Unfortunately, as they approach extinction in the wild, their gene pool shrinks. Inadequate tank filtration, filthy water, or injuries caused by poor tank setup or handling are all symptoms of poor maintenance.

## Careless Handling

Poor care can kill a vulnerable axolotl in captivity. They have specific requirements, including chilly waters, a large tank, and the correct substrate at the bottom of the tank, while being reasonably adaptable compared to other fish. Axolotls should not be handled or taken out of the water due to their delicate body and limbs, as well as their slime covering. The slime coat acts as a barrier against germs and parasites. It may be wiped off with your hands or dried out if the axolotl is removed from the water, so they're a look-but-don't-touch type of pet! Finally, axolotls have been observed to leap from their aquariums. A cover/lid is required to keep them alive and, in the water, where they belong.

## Common diseases

Some of the most common health problems in Axolotls include –

### 1. Ammonia Poisoning

When it comes to your axolotl's health, water quality is critical. Ammonia spikes are toxic to axolotls; therefore, you must often change the water and keep an eye on the toxin levels. Ammonia and nitrite build-up caused by poor tank management will kill your axolotl if left uncontrolled in a matter of days.

Symptoms:

Loss of appetite

Lethargy

Curled and whitened gills
Loss of gills
Red patches on skin
Bleeding

## 2. Hyperthermia

Axolotls like cooler water, and it might be challenging to keep their water cold during the summer heat, but it is vital to avoid hyperthermia. The opposite of hypothermia is hyperthermia. If you keep your axolotl at high temps, it can quickly become overheated. Temperatures exceeding 73 degrees Fahrenheit (23 degrees Celsius) are extremely dangerous because oxygen levels in the tank drop and germs grow, resulting in illnesses.

**Symptoms**

Uncontrollable floating
Loss of appetite
Fluid build-up in the abdomen

## 3. Gastric and Intestinal Foreign Bodies

Impaction is one of the reasons why axolotl rearing manuals advise against using gravel as a substrate for an axolotl tank. Because axolotls eat by sucking in water and whatever food comes with it, there's a reasonable risk they'll swallow large chunks of gravel that won't be digested and cause intestinal blockage. Gravel is preferred to sand or bare-bottom tanks, although even sand can be troublesome for young axolotls. Impaction can also be caused by swallowing tiny fish that barely fit in their jaws. In brief, axolotls are prone to stomach and intestinal problems due to overeating food.

**Symptoms**

- Bloating, constipation, and floating in the tank
- Frantic swimming
- Loss of appetite
- No waste production

## 4. Parasites

Axolotls given live foods are vulnerable to parasitic illnesses brought by live foods. Chances of parasitic illnesses can be considerably reduced by being cautious about where you buy their live meals or developing your own live cultures. Ciliates, Opalina, and Hexamita, as well as protozoa like Costia and Trichodina, can all cause havoc with your axolotls.

**Symptoms**
- Refusal to eat
- Mucus secretion

### 5. Bacterial Infection

Axolotls kept under inadequate tank conditions are prone to bacterial diseases that are easily avoidable. Bacterial infections may be deadly for your axolotls if they are not identified and treated quickly, due to a lack of adequate tank care, contaminated live feeds, or unsterile plants.

**Symptoms**
- Reduced appetite
- Red patches on body
- Fin and tail rot
- Ulcers
- Scale shedding
- Bleeding in the anal and gill area

### 6. Fungus

Extremely high water temperature coupled with bad water conditions are the most common triggers for fungal infections in axolotls.

Symptoms

White, fuzzy patches on body